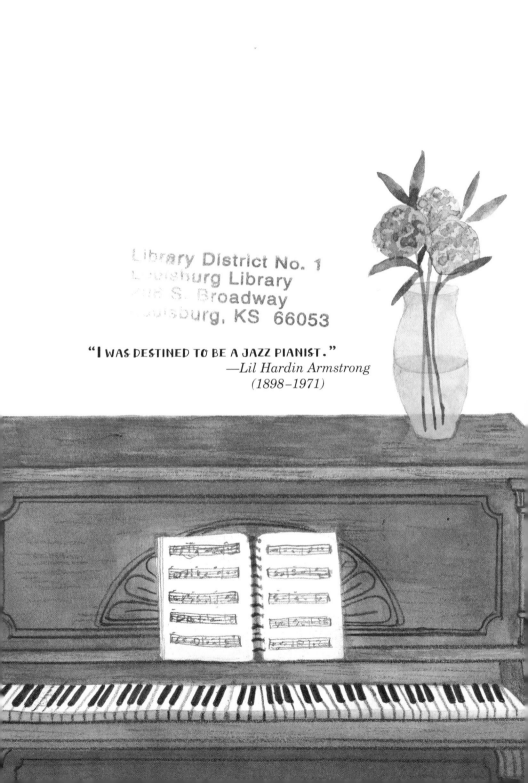

"I WAS DESTINED TO BE A JAZZ PIANIST."
—*Lil Hardin Armstrong*
(1898–1971)

PATRICIA HRUBY POWELL · ILLUSTRATED BY RACHEL HIMES

STRUTTIN' WITH SOME BARBECUE

LIL HARDIN ARMSTRONG BECOMES THE FIRST LADY OF JAZZ

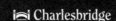

Charlesbridge

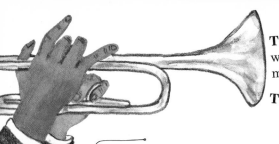

To MORGAN, who plays early jazz with respect and abandon and makes people happy—P. H. P.

To MY PARENTS—R. H.

SPECIAL THANKS TO Dana Hall, Director of Jazz Studies and Associate Professor of Jazz Studies and Ethnomusicology at DePaul University; Mike Miller, tenor banjoist; Ngozi Onuora, Associate Professor at Milliken University's School of Education; and Gabriel Solis, Professor of Music, African American Studies, and Anthropology at the University of Illinois Urbana-Champaign; for their invaluable expertise and advice.

Published by Charlesbridge
85 Main Street
Watertown, MA 02472
(617) 926-0329
www.charlesbridge.com

Library of Congress Cataloging-in-Publication Data
Names: Powell, Patricia Hruby, 1951– author. | Himes, Rachel, illustrator.
Title: Struttin' with some barbecue: Lil Hardin Armstrong becomes the first
    lady of jazz / Patricia Hruby Powell; illustrated by Rachel Himes.
Description: Watertown, MA: Charlesbridge, [2018]
Identifiers: LCCN 2017033092 (print) | LCCN 2017033442 (ebook) | ISBN
    9781632895813 (ebook) | ISBN 9781632895820 (ebook pdf) | ISBN
    9781580897402 (reinforced for library use)
Subjects: LCSH: Armstrong, Lil Hardin, 1898–1971—Juvenile literature. |
    Armstrong, Louis, 1901–1971—Juvenile literature. | Jazz musicians—
    United States—Biography—Juvenile literature.
Classification: LCC ML3930.A747 (ebook) | LCC ML3930.A747 P59 2018
    (print) | DDC 781.65092 [B]—dc23
LC record available at https://lccn.loc.gov/2017033092

Printed in China
(hc) 10 9 8 7 6 5 4 3 2 1

Illustrations created in ink and graphite on hot-pressed Arches paper
Display type set in Meltow Brush
Text type set in Century Schoolbook and Bootstrap
Color separations by Colourscan Print Co Pte Ltd, Singapore
Printed by 1010 Printing International Limited in Huizhou,
    Guangdong, China
Production supervision by Brian G. Walker
Designed by Susan Mallory Sherman and Joyce White

CONTENTS

LIL HARDIN ARMSTRONG

DEAR READER,

I grew up in a musical family, became a concert dancer and choreographer, and married a jazz musician. When I listen to live "traditional" jazz, as early jazz is called, I cannot sit still or keep quiet. I whoop it up when the musicians build to a crescendo. To me, most of the tunes are feel-good music that makes me dance. Even the mournful tunes make me want to *move*.

When my husband, Morgan, suggested I write about Lil Hardin Armstrong, I knew only that she was jazz musician Louis Armstrong's wife and that she was credited with writing some jazz standards—that is, popular jazz tunes. When I started doing research, I totally fell for her—for her gumption, intelligence, drive, and talent. I was astounded that there was so little written about this woman pianist who made it in the man's world of early jazz. That had to change.

So I wrote *Struttin' with Some Barbecue* to celebrate Lil and spotlight her accomplishments. I wanted my words to feel and sound like her jazz tunes—to capture their rhythm, cadence, syncopation, and melody. I threw in surprise words or phrases, just like jazz musicians throw in surprise licks.

In the Louis Armstrong and His Hot Five recordings, you hear Louis yell things like "Ah, whip that thing, Miss Lil!" during the "Gut Bucket Blues" track. These shout-outs and Louis's scat singing (like DEEB DAB DOO dee BUH dee DA BAB) in other tunes inspired me to insert my own bits of scat throughout the story.

I hope my story of the exceptional Lil Hardin Armstrong inspires you to explore early jazz—and makes you want to get up and dance.

—P. H. P.

Lil
memphis, Tenn.

VERSE
Growin' Up in Memphis

STARTING IN 1898

Yessir, Lillian Hardin
was proud to be who she was.
Her mama made sure of that.
Grandma made double sure.

Grandma was a slave—
a bought-and-sold slave—
till the Civil War ended
and she was freed—
free to earn wages
free to raise up her daughter
Dempsey.
Raised her up proud.

Dempsey became Lillian's mama.
She worked as a cook
for a white family
to give Lillian chances
she'd never had.
Lil's daddy was
long gone.

Lil was reared by
Mama and Grandma
in Memphis, Tennessee,
two blocks from
wild, wailin' Beale Street—

where you got

dee-licious

ham, beans, greens

and bar-be-cue

(mm-hmmm)

but also

blues music

juke joints

and pool halls,

yessirree.

All that whoopee worried Mama.

She had a daughter to raise

up right.

1900–1915

At two years old
Lil fiddled around,
fingering the keys
on the rooming-house organ,
her feet dangling
off the bench.
Her cousin stomped on the pedals
below—
making that pump organ
moan, wheeze, and groan.

Mama said,
This girl—
she could be
a piano-playing lady—
a concert pianist.

Yes ma'am,

that's what Mama said,

but bright bold Lil

could make as much music

on an upturned bucket.

Still, Lil learned note reading

and piano playing

thanks to schoolteacher

Miss Violet White.

Lil said,

"I used my fingers any way I wanted."

Sure enough, her fingers went

every which-a-way,

but long as she hit the right notes,

Miss Violet said okay.

At nine,

Lil's feet reached clear to the pedals.

She became the Sunday-school organist

at the Lebanon Baptist Church—

played "Onward, Christian Soldiers"

so it bounced

with a beat so snappy

the kids couldn't help but dance.

Lil just had to dance, too,

sittin' right there at the organ.

Reverend Petty, up in the pulpit,

glared at Lil.

Mama shook her head, said,

Vulgar.

Grandma crossed her arms, said,

Common.

Shucks,

Lil was just followin'

her heart—

or maybe her gut.

'Round about high school
Lil played piano in a recital,
competing for best in her class.
Mama beamed.

Oh no!
Lil lost her place
in the music
but used her noggin
to make a new ending—
improvised it.
The audience thought,
This little girl's so clever—
she's thinking
and making music
at the very same time.

My oh my,
didn't she just bring home
first prize!
WOW za DOO

1915–1916

But Mama worried about
her live-wire
music-lovin' girl
so close to the devil's music—
to Beale Street's
raucous nightlife
gambling
free-flowing corn liquor
scantily clad dancing girls—
so close to
the blues.

Dead in the center of Tennessee
was Nashville—
and Fisk University,
founded to educate
the children of slaves,
to lift them high.

Fisk University
with its grand
classical
elite
music program.
Ju-bi-lee.

Mama insisted that
Lil pack up and ship off
to Fisk—
to play Bach and Brahms
and follow a mess of rules.
Wear a white linen dress—
that was one rule—
also
no walking with boys
no talking to them
don't you go looking at them—
so surely there was
no dancing.

This was no life for Lil.

No fun.

No blues!

She quit Nashville,

hightailed it back to Memphis—

no college degree.

No sirree.

That put Mama in the dumps.

You better believe it.

1916–1917

Strollin' down Beale Street—

center of

her dream—

young

raw

bustin' out

blues—

Lil passed a music shop.

Her eye fixed on
the forbidden
sheet music—
"St. Louis Blues" to be exact—
popular on Beale Street
popular with colored folk.
What folks called "race music."
Work of the devil,
Mama would say,
Not fit for a lady.

Never you mind.

Lil bought that music,
brought it home
and studied it.

When Mama found it
she blew her stack
—beat Lil with a broomstick—
just about beat the devil out of her.

That was the last straw
for Mama.

Lil packed up her bags once again—
Mama did, too.
Bye-bye, Beale Street.

choo-CHOO da
cha-cha CHOOO
Lil and Mama rode the train
to Chicago,
sitting in the
colored car—
separate from white folks—
in those segregated times.

{ 2
C H O R U S
Hot Miss Lil

1917–1919

Lil and Mama set down roots

in the colored

South Side of town—

the Black Belt,

it was called.

That's where

practically all black folks lived—

segregated from white folks.

And one day—

oh, that one day—

steppin' down South State Street,

Lil passed a music store.

She stopped.

Looked once,

looked twice

in that display window

at that forbidden,

oh-so-sinful

—yessir—

sheet music.

In she marched—

small as a child,

prim as a schoolmarm—

to where a man

demonstrated tunes

on the piano,

kinda dull

kinda ho-hum.

Lil sure didn't take to his piano playing.

"Mind letting me try?" she asked.

Nope, didn't mind at all.

Lil sat at that tinklebox and played
like a schoolgirl on fire.
Mrs. Jones, the owner,
liked what she heard
but said, *She's nothing but a child*—
though Lil was twenty.

To Lil, she said,
"Well, honey, if you want to work,
I'll give you three dollars a week."

Three dollars.
Only three dollars?
Well . . .

Back home

Mama just threw up her hands.

'Cause it was gettin'

mighty hard fightin'

high-flyin' Lil.

Besides,

money was money.

So Li'l Ole Girl—

that's what they called her at the shop—

demonstrated music, noon till five

every day.

What she didn't sop up by ear

she sight-read from sheet music

and learned by heart

fast as she could

before Mama could change her mind—

blow the whistle—

stop the job.

That's right.

1919–1920

Jelly Roll Morton up from New Orleans

sauntered into the store.

His long slender fingers hit the ivories hard,

wailin' on the piano—

playin' two rhythms at once

hittin' the offbeat—

that's syncopated.

Oh yeah!

Everybody danced and shouted.

But nobody danced wilder

than Lil,

who near danced outta her skin.

After that

Li'l Ole Girl

put every one

of her eighty-five pounds to work

playin' ferocious

playin' syncopated

playin' like Jelly Roll.

She started changing notes
here and there,
running her fingers up crazy scales,
playing trills.
Dressed like a Sunday-school teacher,
she played hot licks
on the piano.
Dang, she was swingin'
like a gutbucket cat.
Got herself a pay raise—
eight dollars a week.
Everyone, just step aside
'cause here comes
L'il Ole Girl.
STEP da DOO

'Round about then,
the New Orleans Creole Jazz Band
strolled up from the South—
were playing at the Chinese café
over on the West Side—
with no piano player.
Piano players—all men—tried out,
but the band didn't go for 'em.
Mrs. Jones sent
Lil to try out.

Lil asked, "Where's the music?"
They said, "What music?"
"What key do you play in?"
They said, "Key? Just start playing
when you hear two knocks."

Two what?

Knock knock—

Lil banged hard on the keys,

lots of notes,

no particular chord.

But she found her way by ear—

improvising—

playing the changes

the band played.

They hired Li'l Ole Girl

—by golly—

hired a woman to play in a man band.

Girls might sing

but they didn't play piano with the men.

'Cept for Little Ole Lil.

The band moved

to the best cabaret in town—

the Dreamland—

a black-and-tan club,

meaning

a club run by blacks
with entertainment by blacks
and a mostly black audience,
just a few whites coming now and then.

Colored folk
stomped and jived
to the crazy beat of
Lil's piano.
And in no time at all
Lil went from being
Li'l Ole Girl
to Hot
Miss
Lil.

When Mama found out
about the band
she blew her top.
Blew it bad.

"The very *idea*,
as hard as I've worked
to make a lady out of you,
you're playing at a filthy cabaret.
Nothing but vulgar music!"

Mama stormed over
to the cabaret.

Band manager Shaw
greeted Mama like
she was the Queen of Sheba.
"So you are Lillian's mother!
Oh, she is such a nice little girl.
You should be so proud of her."

Still hammerin' away
on the piano,
Lil saw Mama's chest
swell up
with pride.

Mr. Shaw kept on,
"In no time at all,
she'll have the world
at her feet."

When Lil finished the tune
the crowd clapped,
stomped,
all-out cheered
for her.

Under the weight of that thunderous applause
Mama backed down.
Yep, Hot Miss Lil
could go to town
poundin' the keys
rockin' the joint.
But when the clock struck one,
Mama was there at the cabaret door
to fetch her li'l ole girl
home.
Each and every night.

1920–1921

King Joe Oliver
had blown into the Windy City
up from New Orleans.
He'd heard all about
Hot Miss Lil.
Lil lil lil
li'l ole girl

King offered Lil
one hundred dollars a week
to play in his band.
So she gave notice
at the Dreamland
and joined King Oliver's Creole Jazz Band
at the Royal Gardens—
another black-and-tan.
She joined Joe Oliver
'cause he was the King.

Besides which, one hundred dollars was

an awful lot of scratch for anybody,

but a boatload for a girl.

Now

Lil could buy herself some real nice togs,

'cause she liked to dress sharp,

and it meant

ice cream

whenever she wanted,

which was pretty often.

WHOOP de DOO

After playing Chicago for a spell

the band took off

for San Francisco

to a white club—

the Pergola Ballroom.

But what d'ya know—

the white folks out west
couldn't dance to the beat
'cause the colored musicians were hittin'
the offbeats
—two and four—
the New Orleans way
and those white dancers were hittin'
regular ole
one and three.
Yep.

Lil, the brains of the band,
saw what was happenin'—
but what was there to do?
This was a new form of music
up from New Orleans—
folks called it
jazz.

The white crowd just couldn't cut the rug

to the newfangled music,

so the band flopped.

No more gigs.

No more work.

No money.

They rolled back to raucous, raw Chicago

and played at the Royal Gardens

where the colored folk

swayed, shimmied, and strutted

to that *jazz* music—

that colored music—

dancin' right outta this world.

Two and four, baby.

3
B L O W I N '
Enter Louis

1922

Shortly after that,

King Oliver sent for

young Louis Armstrong

down in New Orleans—

Dippermouth, they called him

'cause his mouth was wide as a

water dipper—

to play second trumpet

behind the King's

first trumpet.

Yeah!

Now, all the band members
were sweet on pretty Lil,
but Lil took off each night
with her mama
soon as the gig finished.
Didn't even know the players
were sweet on her.

So much for that.
King Oliver went and told Lil
that little Louis
was sweet on her.
Well, fine.

But Lord-A'mighty.
Lil looked at Louis
dressed threadbare,
talkin' backwoods,
bangs hangin'
over his forehead,
like a country boy
from swamp country.

40

Yep, that's where he came from.
New Orleans bayou—
the Delta—
small town.

And why'd they call him "little Louis,"
she wanted to know.
The short hick from the bayou
weighed in at 226 pounds.

He was too country
too backwater
too bumpkin
for a sophisticated gal like
Hot Miss Lil.

But King also said
Louis could play
better
than he could.

Louis play better
than the King?

That sparked Lil's interest.

But how was she supposed to hear Louis

when he was standing

right behind the King,

playing in and around

the same melody line?

One night

she set her ear real close-like

to the bell of Louis's horn

and listened hard.

Yep,

pretty tone

clear as water,

played straight from his heart—

almost like he was singin'.

BETta BETta

BOP pa DOO

Then King said to Lil,

"Long as I keep him second to me

he won't get ahead of me.
I'll still be the King."

Now that just wasn't right.

Lil kept listenin' close,
heard Louis's story
in that sweet clear sound—
'bout bumpin' around
Storyville,
rough tough New Orleans.

She heard
those troubles get turned to a smirk
then widen to a smile
all the way to a laugh.
Yeah, baby.

Lil got to likin' Louis's wide
dippermouth smile—
big as his heart
big as his belly.

They began steppin' out together—
went on a date.
And another.
The band didn't even know about it.

Lo and behold,
King got sick for a spell.
Lil got to hear Louis blow
his horn
out front—first trumpet.
Everyone heard him
clear and clean
playin' like a lion
leapin' and roarin'
playin' from that big ole heart of his.

The band was solid
as the Rock of Gibraltar—

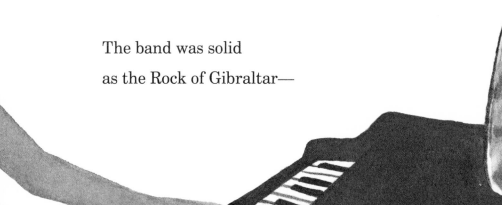

Lil at the piano
pumpin' her arms
tappin' her feet
groundin' the beat.
The others swingin' and swayin'
playin' off each other
and Louis adding in surprise—
changin' the tempo
improvisin' a solo—
and Baby Dodds on drums
following his lead.

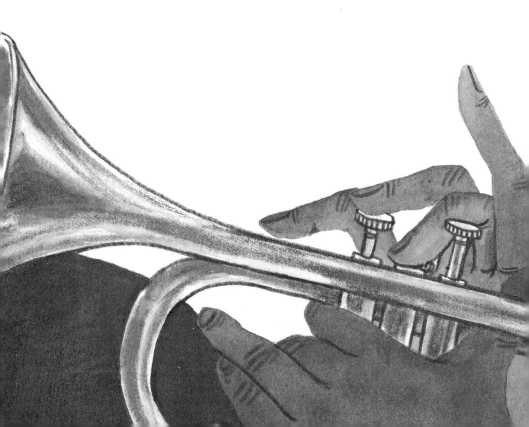

King Oliver came back.

Louis went back to playing second,

but now Louis—he'd been

heard out front.

HOO HAH

White players strolled in

from across town

to the South Side—

came listening

and admiring

the band's hot music—

wanted to pick up some of them

red-hot licks

Louis played.

Fact was

Louis, Lil, and the band

were makin' a new language

tellin' their sorrows in their music—

about growin' up poor,

a generation or two away from being

slaves—

but flippin' it around

makin' that pain something else

easing those hard times

makin' folks wanna dance

wanna laugh

wanna shout for joy.

Glory be!

LATER IN 1922

Lil, in the money,
doing the thing
she loved to do—
what she was born to do,
play *jazz*—
bought herself a secondhand Hudson car
'bout a block long
(called it a short).
Mostly people rode the streetcar.
A girl drivin' a car looked kinda wild.
Lil liked that.

She took Louis for a joyride
along with King Joe Oliver
on hustlin' bustlin' Michigan Avenue—
with cars and buggies runnin'
every which-a-way.
Right in the middle of traffic
the short stalled—
wouldn't start.

Cars tooted. Drivers shouted,

Outta the way!

Move that heap!

A stranger got out of his own car

got into Lil's

started it up.

Yes oh yes. Thank you, sir.

The three drove off,

hot-faced

but laughin'

through a mess of honkin'

and shoutin'.

Louis was a shy guy—

didn't go for that mess-up.

He told Lil, "If you want to go out with me

we'll have to walk or get on the streetcar."

So next time they hopped onto a streetcar

and rolled down the street

to a show,

then a dance,

sweetheartin' all the way.

On the bandstand

Lil's heart pounded clear through her

arms to her hands

to the ivories.

She played her all for Louis.

And Louis blew up a storm for his Lil.

The band saw

that Lil was stuck on Louis

and stopped talkin' to 'em both

for a spell—

till they started teasing Louis,

saying

50

the bayou bumpkin
won city-smart Lil.
That's right.

Lil and Louis
out on a date
climbed onto a streetcar.
Louis grabbed high for the bar,
his threadbare jacket
pullin' so tight
it 'bout burst at the seams.
Lil could hold back no longer—
"You've got to change your clothes.
Where's your money?"

Louis's jaw dropped clear to his chest.
He sputtered,
"Mister Joe keeps my money."
Lord-A'mighty, he called King Oliver
"Mr. Joe."
"He sent for me and he looks out for me."

Lil said, "You keep your own money.
I'm going to look out for you from now on."

And she did.

If Lil could dress sharp as a tack,
why so could a boyfriend.
Wasn't that right?

Lil marched downtown, bought Louis
a velour hat and a trim overcoat.
Yessir.
She dressed him snappy.

Louis ate ribs.
Lil told him he'd be better off
eating vegetables.
Louis grumbled.
But he listened.
Sometimes.

Now Louis's mama, Mayann,
come up from
Storyville, New Orleans—
to check on that boy of hers
'cause she heard he wasn't doing
too good.

Fact was, Louis was doin'
better than good.

Louis and Lil were earnin'
a boatload of money—
playin' jazz.
Believe it, baby.

Lil left her mama's house
and rented an apartment with Louis.
Lil decorated it swanky—
new chairs
new tables
new beds.
WHOOP de DOO

They invited Mayann to come along
and live with 'em.
When Mayann saw all that luxury
she was so flabbergasted
tears ran down her cheeks.
Which made Louis
love Lil
all the more—
pleasin' his mama like that.

54

Lil loved pleasin' Louis.

1923

King's band took a train to
Richmond, Indiana,
to huddle around a
recording machine—
looked like a tin lily.

Louis's chops were good
and he played loud—
way louder than King Oliver.
They told Louis to back up
back up
back up
fifteen feet from the tin lily.

Lil felt bad for Louis,

so far from the band—

lookin' so lonesome,

kinda sad

kinda funny.

NEVer oh EVer

you MIND.

Each one of the musicians

earned thirty bucks per tune.

Nine tracks.

That sure was a lotta loot.

But it was so new—

this recording thing.

Had they done right?

Or had they gone and

given their music away?

Maybe so.

Maybe not.

After all day

in the hot studio,

playin' track after track,

the band had no place to stay

at night

in that Ku Klux Klan hotbed—

Richmond.

They stayed up and took

the early-morning

milk train

back to Chicago.

4
HOT ENSEMBLE OUT
To the Top, Baby

1924

Lil and Louis—

both playin' their hearts out

in the top jazz band in the world,

in love—

got married.

That's solid, baby.

On gigs together

Lil heard

Louis play stuff

no one had ever played

before—

but dang if he still wasn't

playin' second to the King.

Now that just wouldn't do.

No way,

no how.

At home

Lil listened to Louis

whistlin' out his story,

turnin' those hard ole times

into deep riffs,

flippin' those memories into laughin' trills,

makin' music

so fine

she wanted to

dance and shout.

Out on the back step

Lil sang.

Louis whistled.

Makin' music—
that's how they thought,
how they talked.
Lil, with her top-notch note knowledge,
wrote it down—
penned "Jazz Lips"
and "Skid-Dat-De-Dat."
Louis could read and write music,
but not as well as Lil.
Lil helped Louis
turn his riffs and trills
into written notes—
and improve his reading.

Lil—
raised up
by Mama and Grandma
to aim for the stars—
was ready to show
Louis that same thing.

While penning a new tune
she laid down her pencil,
said,
"If you're gonna stay with me
you'll have to play first trumpet."

"Well what do you want me to do?"
Louis asked.

"I want you to give notice."

Ooh, it was scary to quit the band,
quit that nice fat paycheck.
But Louis did it.
He knew Lil was right.

Lil stayed on

'cause someone had to

make some dough.

LATER IN 1924

Now that they were married,

Lil's mama,

she moved in, too.

Both mamas,

Louis and Lil,

all shared digs—

shared a home.

Worked out swell for everyone

having all that extra family around.

But Louis needed work.

He asked Sammy Stewart

for a gig in his orchestra.

Sammy snapped, *No.*

Didn't need no trumpeter.

Louis near 'bout crawled under a rock.

Scared Lil, too,
but she didn't let on.
Weeks passed.
No work.
She said to Louis,
"Pretty soon he'll be eating at your feet."

Well, what do ya know?
Ollie Powers offered Louis a place
in his band.
Whew.

So Louis played his horn
out front,
first trumpet—
only trumpet.
Now we're talkin'.

Lil's li'l ole push
was just the thing Louis needed
to set him climbin'.

Next thing you know,
Fletcher Henderson asked Louis
to come out
to New York City—
play in his band.
Now we're rollin'.

Lil sent Louis off
with kisses
and good wishes.

In New York
Louis blew.
He cooked.
He wailed on his horn—
not just in Fletcher's band
but other gigs, too.
His reputation grew
day by day—
that squat cat
still burstin' at the seams.

Lil joined him in New York,
but Fletcher didn't need
a piano player—
no sir.
He played piano.

On top of that
no one knew Miss Lil
in New York.
No one appreciated her
hot style.

Jazz—as Lil knew it—

came straight up the Mississippi

from New Orleans, through Memphis.

Landed—still earthy

unschooled

colorful

raw—

in Chicago.

Lil learned it like that,

playin' on the bandstand.

Out east in New York,

players studied

that sound—

but played it

slick and flashy

with real good tone.

They sounded kinda mechanical

alongside Lil's

rough and ready approach.

You play it, Lil.

So all the time Louis was soaring,

Lil was going nowhere.

She stood

real lonely-like

at the bottom of the ladder,

watching Louis climb

up

up

up.

But still,

Louis was playin' in somebody else's band.

His name wasn't

written out

anywhere—

not on the marquee

not on the bandstand

not in the program.

1925

Lil had a plan—
hightailed it back home,
where they,
the jazz couple,
could play together
in the raw, happenin' Chicago scene,
where cabarets were run
by the underworld,
where people knew her
and knew Louis
both—
and their hot playin'.

Lil booked a new band
at the Dreamland—
told Louis,
"Come on back home.
I've got a job for you."

Louis just wanted to blow his horn
and worry 'bout nothin'.
He was no ambitious cat.

Lil,
ambitious enough for the both of 'em
and wanting her husband in Chicago,
said,
"Come now or don't come at all."

That did it.
Louis chose Lil.

And Lil was true to her word.
A banner flew over the Dreamland:

MADAME LIL ARMSTRONG'S
DREAMLAND SYNCOPATORS
FEATURING
Louis Armstrong,
THE WORLD'S GREATEST TRUMPET PLAYER

Louis said, "Girl, are you crazy?"

Shy Louis didn't like all that attention—

but Louis *was* the greatest trumpet player.

Lil knew

that deep down,

Louis cared about

being the great trumpet player

she knew

he was.

At gigs,

Louis ended a tune

on a

high F.

No one else could do that.

Every night the cats waited for that

high F.

Folks came out just to hear that

high F.

Louis worried he'd miss that dang

high F.

Lil told him he better

woodshed on that F—

practice blowin' higher.

Make that F easy.

Out on the back step,

Louis blew

G after G.

Lil was right, yessirree.

Now that high F

was in the pocket.

Louis took

some crazy journeys on his trumpet,

dippin'

turnin'

hittin' that high F.

The whole band—

they were playin' feel-good music.

And folks just kept pourin' in to listen.

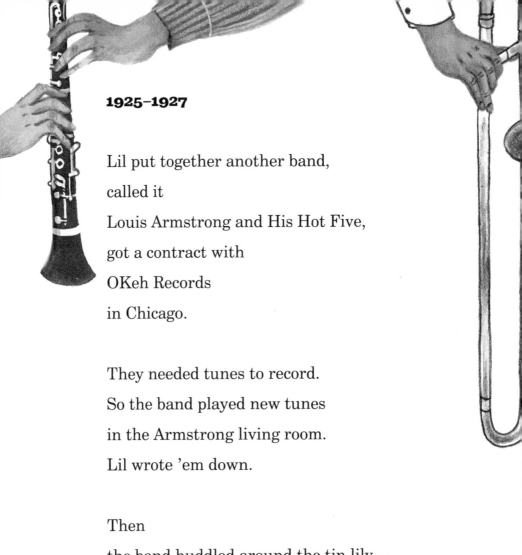

1925–1927

Lil put together another band,
called it
Louis Armstrong and His Hot Five,
got a contract with
OKeh Records
in Chicago.

They needed tunes to record.
So the band played new tunes
in the Armstrong living room.
Lil wrote 'em down.

Then
the band huddled around the tin lily—
Louis on trumpet
Lil on piano

Kid Ory slidin' on trombone
Johnny Dobbs on clarinet
and Johnny St. Cyr on banjo,
sittin' high up on a ladder
to get the balance
right.

They cut another record.
Zop a wha DO

Lil, Louis,
and the Hot Five
were makin'
jazz.
I'm tellin' ya.

They recorded "Heebie Jeebies."

Some folks say Louis forgot the words,

but maybe he just felt like

scattin'—

makin' up sounds as he went along—

SCEEP SCAM SKIP *oh dee* **DAT** *de* **DOO**

Back at the cabaret

the band was smokin'

hotter than usual,

and Louis hit an even higher note.

Lil beamed.

After the gig

Lil told him what he hit—

not an F, not a G—

a high C.

YA ZOO *la*

More folks

came out to hear

the band.

Lil pounded the keys,

Louis blew his horn

scatted

joked

sometimes did a little crazy dance.

Louis dropped his shy.

Maybe Lil's confidence made him brave.

Maybe the music made him high—

whatever—

couldn't be nothin' more excitin'.

All the time

Lil was teaching Louis

to read notes—

read music—

better and better.

Lil wrote "Lonesome Blues"

and "King of the Zulus."

She wrote "Struttin' with Some Barbecue"—

her best—

yessir.

So joyous a strut,

so light a touch,

so fine a tune

it was played

over and over—

not just by Louis and Lil—

but by loads and loads

of bands,

'cause playin' it

and hearin' it

feels like

taking a get-happy tonic.

Zop a wha DO

Lil and Louis

were struttin' high on the hog

right there in Chicago,

up from the South,

makin'

raw and raucous

rompin', rollickin'

music.

Dang, they were musical royalty—
inventing
a new kind of sound—
makin'
jazz.

And Lil,
well, Lil was a lady all right—
just like Mama hoped,
just like Li'l Ole Girl dreamed—
the first lady
of *jazz*.

I'm tellin' ya.

Absolutely,
baby.

AND WHAT'S MORE

A Little About Lil

Tunes composed by Lil Hardin Armstrong are still played today. Besides "Struttin' with Some Barbecue," there's "Oriental Swing"; "Just for a Thrill," which became a hit in 1959 when Ray Charles revived it; and "Bad Boy," which Ringo Starr revived in 1978.

In Lil's day there were female jazz vocalists, but Lil was one of the very few female instrumentalists. Being a respected band member playing with the men was a feat in itself. But Lil was playing with the best jazz musicians of the age—King Oliver and his band, and of course, Louis Armstrong.

Lil was not only a pioneer of jazz music, but also a star maker. Today Louis (usually pronounced *LOO-ee*) Armstrong is considered the first great jazz trumpet soloist. There are those who say that Louis would never have been the star he became if it weren't for Lil pushing him to the front. She was ambitious enough to drive both herself and Louis. But that driving was hard on the marriage, as was Louis's infidelity. Lil and Louis divorced in 1938. Louis married a few more times, but Lil never did.

Lil played jazz her whole life—in Chicago, New York, and Europe. Along the way, she trained to become a clothing designer—and made suits and shirts for Louis. In time she went back to classical music, studying at the Chicago Musical College. She played recitals of Mozart, Weber, Chopin, Debussy, and Scriabin.

Louis and Lil remained friends for life. A month after Louis died in August 1971, Lil was playing a memorial concert for him in Chicago when she collapsed at the piano. She died on the way to the hospital.

Jazz Notes

At the beginning of the twentieth century, both blues and jazz (or jass, as it was first called) were known as "race music"—having originated in the black community with the descendants of slaves. The roots of jazz include gospel singing, ragtime, field chants, and brass bands. At the turn of the twentieth century, artists were mixing Creole, Caribbean, Mexican, and African American musical ideas in the port city of New Orleans. By the 1920s, with southern black musicians migrating north, Chicago had become the center of jazz, helped along by the recordings made there. It's true that musicians were often reluctant to record, wondering if they were giving—or even throwing—their music away. The contrary proved to be true. Although other musicians listened to the records and tried to replicate the music, the records proved who played it first. Thanks to the recordings, we can still hear and appreciate Lil, Louis, the Hot Five, and other outstandingly talented individuals who produced great music together.

Today jazz is considered by many to be the only original American art form.

Black and Tan and White Times

Lil and the band endured the segregation of the times, particularly when on the road. Black travelers sat in the train car for "coloreds," which was not kept clean by the railroad staff like the white car was. The band could not stay overnight in Richmond, Indiana, where the white supremacist Ku Klux Klan had a stronghold. In other "sundown" towns they probably had to hide when night fell. However, Lil does not speak of racism in her existing interviews, so we don't know how it affected her personally.

For the most part, early jazz bands were segregated, as were their audiences. However, white players (and some white fans) came to Chicago's South Side clubs in order to hear and study the jazz played by Lil, Louis, and other great black musicians. (Likewise, whites in New York visited Harlem to hear jazz.) Jazz was a black art form, which whites were listening to, studying, and adopting. But not all whites were ready for this new sound, as Lil and King Oliver's Creole Jazz Band found out in San Francisco. Most white jazz musicians (as well as some black musicians) opted to play "sweet" jazz, which was softer and less raucous than Lil and Louis's "hot" jazz and involved little or no improvisation. "Sweet" jazz was more accepted by white audiences due to its being closer to the popular white music they knew.

Despite this divergence in style, historians like Alain Locke claim that jazz was a "great interracial collaboration" originating with black players. Players of both races admired players of the other race. As is true today, the arts tend to be a melting pot of ideas—because artists are often more concerned with art than with skin color or cultural differences.

Coda

After Lil's funeral, her house was pilfered of
her letters, the manuscript of her unpublished
autobiography, her photographs, and other personal
effects. These items have never been found. Any
heirs of Lil's would be owed a good deal of money in
royalties, but they have not been found either. Their
surnames would probably be Hardin or Martin, and
it is likely that they would be living in northern
Mississippi or western Tennessee.

If you're wondering why Lil's grandmother,
Priscilla Martin, disappears from the story, it's because
she disappears from the historical record. She most
likely died between the census years of 1900 and 1910.
And what about Lil's father, William Hardin? Lil said
he'd died when she was two, but the census shows a
William Hardin living at various addresses in Memphis
in the 1900 and 1910 censuses, and no death certificate
has been found in the county.

TIME LINE

February 3, 1898: Lillian Hardin born in Memphis, Tennessee, to Dempsey and William Hardin.

1915–1916: Attends Fisk University in Nashville, Tennessee.

1917 or 1918: Moves to Chicago with Dempsey and Dempsey's new husband, John Miller.

1921: Joins King Oliver's Creole Jazz Band.

1922: Marries aspiring singer Jimmy Johnson and divorces him shortly after. Louis Armstrong joins King Oliver's Creole Jazz Band.

1923: Records with King Oliver's Creole Jazz Band.

1924: Marries Louis Armstrong.

1925–1927: Records with Louis Armstrong and His Hot Five.

1928: Earns a degree from Chicago Musical College; plays concert of Chopin and Debussy.

1930s: Heads the All Girl Orchestra and another big band. Records for Decca as a swing music vocalist. Lil and Louis live apart.

1938: Divorces Louis Armstrong, but they remain friends for life.

1940s and 1950s: Appears in the Broadway shows *Hot Chocolates* and *Shuffle Along*. Returns to Chicago and works as a soloist, singing and playing piano. Trains as a tailor and becomes a clothing designer. Performs in Europe.

1960s: Records sporadically and performs, mostly in Chicago.

July 6, 1971: Louis Armstrong dies.

August 27, 1971: While playing "St. Louis Blues" in a commemorative performance for Louis, Lil suffers a stroke and dies.

GLOSSARY

blow: to play a musical instrument.

blow your top: to get angry; to go crazy.

cat: a jazz musician or aficionado, or a regular person.

chops: the lips and surrounding muscles, or a
musician's technique.

colored: black, African American. Now an
offensive term.

cut the rug: to dance.

digs: home.

dough: money.

gig: a musician's performance, or a performer's job at
a club or cabaret.

gutbucket: earthy. Louis Armstrong named a tune
"Gut Bucket Blues." When he was asked what "gut
bucket" meant, he said he just made it up. But
band member Johnny St. Cyr explained that in
New Orleans, fishmongers slit open fish and raked
their guts into a bucket. *That's* "gutbucket"—
low-down blues.

happenin': lively; hip.

in the pocket: easily attainable.

ivories: piano keys.

juke joint: a music club or cabaret, usually with dancing, drinking, and perhaps eating.

lick: a musical phrase, or series of notes.

loot: money.

milk train: a slow local train, which sometimes actually delivered milk.

newfangled: of the newest style.

noggin: head.

Queen of Sheba: a big-deal person; someone to make a fuss over. From the tenth-century BCE monarch of the kingdom of Sheba, thought to be in Ethiopia or Yemen.

race music: music from the African American community, as it was called by both whites and blacks in the 1920s.

riff: a musical phrase or passage.

rock: to rouse to excitement; to energize.

scat: to sing nonsense syllables (like *YA ZOO la* or *Zop a wha DO*), or the nonsense syllables themselves.

scratch: money.

solid: solidly good.

steppin' out: going out on a date.

swanky: expensive and showy; stylish.

syncopated: stressing a normally weak beat.

tinklebox: piano.

togs: clothes.

wail: to play in an intense or inspired manner.

whoopee: merrymaking.

woodshed: to practice intensely in solitude— as in out in a woodshed.

KEEPIN' UP WITH LIL

Further Resources and Selected Bibliography

While researching and writing this book, I drew upon interviews, books, articles, and websites—and of course Lil's music itself. Check out the sources below.

FOR YOUNGER READERS

Armstrong, Lil Hardin. "An Audio Interview with Lil Hardin Armstrong." By Chris Albertson. *Stomp Off!* (blog). August 31, 2010. http://stomp-off.blogspot.com /2010/08/lil-armstrong-interview-1-of-2.html. Three-part series.

Armstrong, Lil Hardin. "Lil Hardin Armstrong, 1957." Interview in *And They All Sang: Adventures of an Eclectic Disc Jockey*, 139–44. Edited by Studs Terkel. New York: New Press, 2005.

Armstrong, Lil Hardin. "Lil Hardin Interview Clips." *Stanford University Libraries: The Jim Cullum Riverwalk Jazz Collection*. Clips from the 1956 Riverside LP *Satchmo and Me: Lil Armstrong's Own Story*. http://rwj-a.stanford.edu/bonus-content /lil-hardin-interview-clips.

Dickerson, James L. *Just for a Thrill: Lil Hardin Armstrong, First Lady of Jazz*. New York: Cooper Square Press, 2002.

Pick, Margaret Moos. "Behind Every Great Man: Lil Hardin and Louis Armstrong." *Stanford University Libraries: The Jim Cullum Riverwalk Jazz Collection.* 2012. http://riverwalkjazz.stanford.edu/program /behind-every-great-man-lil-hardin-and-louis-armstrong.

Shapiro, Nat, and Nat Hentoff. *Hear Me Talkin' to Ya: The Story of Jazz as Told by the Men Who Made It.* New York: Rinehart, 1955.

FOR OLDER READERS

Armstrong, Lil Hardin. "Satchmo and Me." *American Music* 25, no. 1 (Spring 2007), 106–118. www.jstor.org/stable/40071645.

Armstrong, Louis. *Swing That Music.* New York: Da Capo Press, 1993.

Collier, James Lincoln. *Louis Armstrong: An American Genius.* New York: Oxford University Press, 1983.

Jones, Max, and John Chilton. *Louis: The Louis Armstrong Story, 1900–1971.* Boston: Little, Brown, 1971.

Kenney, William Howland. *Chicago Jazz: A Cultural History, 1904–1930.* New York: Oxford University Press, 1993.

Locke, Alain. *The Negro and His Music.* Washington, DC: The Associates in Negro Folk Education, 1936. http://babel.hathitrust.org/cgipt?id=mdp .39015009742886;view=1up;seq=92.

Seago, Lynne. "From Potent to Popular: The Effects of Racism on Chicago Jazz 1920–1930." *Constructing the Past* 1 (2000). http://digitalcommons.iwu.edu/cgi /viewcontent.cgi?article=1069&context=constructing.

Teachout, Terry. *Pops: A Life of Louis Armstrong.* Boston: Houghton Mifflin Harcourt, 2009.

THE TUNES

Armstrong, Lil Hardin. *Chicago: The Living Legends: Lil Hardin Armstrong and Her Orchestra.* Riverside, 1993, compact disc. Originally recorded in 1961–1970.

Armstrong, Lil Hardin. *Lil Hardin Armstrong and Her Swing Orchestra 1936–1940.* Classics Records, 1991, compact disc. Originally recorded in 1936–1940.

Armstrong, Louis. *Hot Fives and Sevens.* JSP Records, 2002, four compact discs. Originally recorded in 1925– ca. 1929. (Includes "Struttin' with Some Barbecue.")

Oliver, King. *I'll Still Be King.* Featuring Louis Armstrong, Johnny Dodds, Lil Hardin, Barney Bigard, and J. C. Higginbotham. Fabulous, 2005, streaming audio. Originally recorded in 1923–1930. http://www .allmusic.com/album/ill-still-be-king-mw0001346586.

The URLs listed here were accurate at publication, but websites often change. If a URL doesn't work, you can use the internet to find more information.

QUOTATION SOURCES

For more information about the sources below, see the selected bibliography on pages 89–91.

PAGE 1: "I was destined . . . jazz pianist": Lil Hardin Armstrong, "Lil Hardin Armstrong, 1957," p. 144.

PAGE 13: "I used my . . . I wanted": Lil Hardin Armstrong, "Satchmo and Me," p. 108.

PAGE 24: "Mind letting me try?": Lil Hardin Armstrong, "Lil Hardin Armstrong, 1957," p. 140.

PAGE 25: "Well, honey, . . . a week": Jennie Jones quoted by Lil Hardin Armstrong in "Lil Hardin Armstrong, 1957," p.140.

PAGE 29: "Where's the music?" conversation: Reported by Lil Hardin Armstrong in "Lil Hardin Armstrong, 1957," p. 141. Actual quote:
Lil: Where's the music?
Band: Music? We haven't got any music.
We don't use any.
Lil: Well, what key are you going to play in?
Band: When you hear two knocks, you just start playing.

PAGE 32: "The very *idea* . . . vulgar music!": Dempsey Hardin quoted by Lil Hardin Armstrong in "Lil Hardin Armstrong, 1957," p. 142.

PAGE 32: "So you are . . . proud of her": Izzy Shaw quoted by Lil Hardin Armstrong in "Lil Hardin Armstrong, 1957," p. 142.

PAGE 33: "In no time . . . her feet": Ibid.

PAGES 42-43: "Long as I . . . the King": Joe "King" Oliver quoted by Lil Hardin Armstrong in "Satchmo and Me," p. 112. Actual quote: "But as long as I keep him with me he won't be able to get ahead of me. I'll still be the King."

PAGE 50: "If you want . . . the streetcar": Louis Armstrong quoted by Lil Hardin Armstrong in "Satchmo and Me," p. 113.

PAGES 51-52: "You've got to change your clothes" conversation: Reported by Lil Hardin Armstrong in "Satchmo and Me," p. 113. Actual quote:
  Lil: You've got to change your clothes.
  Louis: What's the matter with my clothes? . . .
  Lil: Where's your money?
  Louis: Well, Joe keeps my money.
  Lil: Well, Joe doesn't need to keep your money. You keep your own money. You go to Joe and get your money.
  Louis: Well, I'd rather for Mister Joe—
  Lil (to interviewer): He called him Mister Joe, you know—
  Louis: I'd rather Mister Joe, you know. He sent for me and looks out for me.
  Lil: No, I'm going to look out for you from now on.

PAGE 62: "If you're gonna stay with me" conversation: Reported by Lil Hardin Armstrong in "Satchmo and Me," p. 114. Actual quote:
  Lil: If you're gonna stay with me you'll have to play first.
  Louis: Well what do you want me to do?
  Lil: I want you to give him a notice.

PAGE 64: "Pretty soon . . . your feet": Lil Hardin Armstrong, "Satchmo and Me," p. 115.

PAGE 70: "Come on . . . job for you": Lil Hardin Armstrong, "Satchmo and Me," p. 116.

PAGE 71: "Come now or don't come at all": Ibid. Actual quote: "If you're not here by this date, then don't come at all."

PAGE 72: "Girl, are you crazy?": Louis Armstrong quoted by Lil Hardin Armstrong in "Satchmo and Me," p. 116.

PAGE 84: "great interracial collaboration": Locke, p. 82.

INDEX